The Cats' House

The Cats' House
5010 Northaven Avenue
San Diego, CA 92110
www.catshouse.com

Tyler Blik Design
655 G Street, Suite E
San Diego, CA 92101
www.tylerblik.com

National Cat Protection Society
6904 W. Coast Highway
Newport Beach, CA 92663
www.natcat.org

ISBN-13: 978-0-7407-7861-2
ISBN-10: 0-7407-7861-7

Library of Congress Control Number:
2008935761

09 10 11 12 13 SDB 10 9 8 7 6 5 4 3 2 1

www.andrewsmcmeel.com

ATTENTION: SCHOOLS AND BUSINESSES
Andrews McMeel books are available at
quantity discounts with bulk purchase for
educational, business, or sales promotional
use. For information, please write to: Special
Sales Department, Andrews McMeel
Publishing, LLC, 1130 Walnut Street, Kansas
City, Missouri 64106.

The Cats' House

Text and Photographs by
Bob Walker

**Andrews McMeel
Publishing, LLC**

Kansas City

Each day, my wife Frances and I

leave our home in the custody of our nine cat companions.

If possession is nine-tenths of the law, then

our place is truly the cats' house.

What they do with their time only they know.

For several years, our time has been spent altering the house

to satisfy the needs of the cats. We have constructed one hundred and ten feet

of elevated walkway to allow our felines to pass through walls and frolic overhead.

Home is definitely where the cats roam. They are everywhere: under-foot,

over-foot; on counters, shelves, laps, and furnishings; even in the air above.

Our cats think all cats live this way. We think all cats should.

By making public our private space, we hope others will be encouraged

to create a better existence for their companions.

Cats

Frances and I met while stuffing envelopes for a California political campaign. Unlike myself, she had always lived with cats. We opted for a small courthouse wedding performed by a justice of the peace. Only immediate family and a couple of friends were invited. Very few gifts. Still, we received three Crock-Pots.

No romantic honeymoon was in store for us. Instead, we visited a friend in the late afternoon and adopted Beauregard, a long-haired tabby—a terrific start, our first cat for our new home.

We quickly discovered that Beauregard needed a playmate. When left unattended, he would be forced to entertain himself. Like a master chef, Beauregard could skillfully combine our kitchen's ingredients into his own fun activities—like the day he removed the macaroni noodles from their cupboard and swatted them hockey-style throughout the house; or the times he transferred wet dish rags from the kitchen sink onto our living room couch. (Eventually, we learned to tie the dish rags to the faucet.)

of
Character

Frances and I answered a newspaper ad to find Beauregard's new playmate. Overwhelmed with a bathtub full of "they're all adorable" Siamese kittens, we decided on the guy that purred the most. Everyone loved Benjamin. He was the kind of cat who welcomed all to his home. If you needed to pet a cat, Benjamin was always willing.

Immediately, Benjamin and Beauregard became the best of friends—and, thankfully, our kitchen experienced far less of Beauregard than before. But neither Frances nor I could have imagined what incredible changes would be in store for us by becoming a more-than-one-cat family.

Our Extended Family

Since Beauregard and Benjamin first entered our lives . . . Frances and I have shared over twenty years of marriage, several moves of residence, and an insatiable fondness/weakness for kittens/cats.

Each spring, we make our pilgrimage to the National Cat Protection Society's shelter to inspect the new crop of kittens. Frances and I have discovered that we're usually attracted to the orphan cats with questionable lineage. (There's always a little bit of every cat in a mixed breed.) Invariably, we fall in love with another kitty and, of course, home it comes—once more expanding our family of feline companions.

TomCat is a good example of why orange tabbies are called marmalade cats—he's as sweet as jelly. Tom licks visitors' fingers until they are perfectly clean, then he bites their fingers (not hard, just love-bites). Mom must have told young Tom never to bite anything unless it's been washed first.

When Jerry Lee was a kitten, he would not let sleeping cats lie. Jerry knew that if he attacked while they were napping he would be in a better position to win during the struggles that always followed.

Calafia is a cat of many colors. It's always a special honor when she selects our laps for her naps. We believe her aloofness is retribution for selecting her on appearance alone. Once again it proves: You can't judge a cat by its spots.

Jerry Lee needed a playmate. Celeste was just the right kitten. Frances adopted her from our favorite shelter. Our new girl was affectionate, had distinctive black-and-white markings, and, most importantly, possessed boundless energy.

Joseph is the opposite of Calafia. He needs to be the center of attention. Bring out a camera, he's ready to pose. Ready to feed a cat or provide a lap for a nap? Joseph must be first.

Our guys thought we'd brought home a real feline femme fatale. Denise's beautiful patches of orange, black, and white captured their attention— and ours, too. However, her spots have been spreading lately. Our vet says that Denise has fat cells. We prefer to think of her as our big-boned calico gal.

Cats of Character

Simon was one of those darling little kittens that couldn't be resisted. He purred, played, and had looks, too— a true trophy cat. We knew our friends would be jealous if we had a cat like that. Once home, however, he was a little shy. When visitors arrived, Simon would hide until they left.

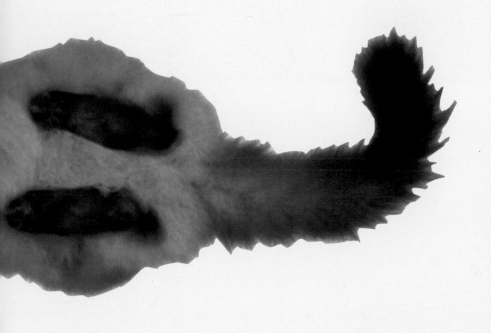

At the shelter, an affectionate little guy with sweet, round eyes and a butter-ball body tried to stow away in Frances's purse. How could we resist? Bernard will always be our baby. He has the markings and body of a killer whale but is as lovable as a teddy bear.

Friends of ours found Terri abandoned at a grocery store. Six months after she had been orphaned and then adopted into our home, Terri passed away. With each setback we were reminded of how limited our efforts can be—how ephemeral the special gift of life truly is. Terri was loving—and loved—to the very end.

Frank-the-Friendly-Kitten is our "Welcoming Cat." He approaches everyone tail-fluffed-and-straight. But we must always caution dinner guests: Frank's neighborly gestures can be deceptive. With a quick tail flick, your food can become his.

Molly is the dalmatian that I've always been secretly hoping for. Okay, so she doesn't have as many spots as the dog version. (I checked: During the selection process, I lifted her over my head to inspect her spots from underneath.)

How We Introduce New Members

Sometimes, a shelter kitten captivates us head-and-tail above the others. Little Jimmy was playful, affectionate, and he unabashedly meowed to attract our attention. Frances and I named him after the four-foot eleven-inch Country Music Hall of Famer "Little" Jimmy Dickens, who sang the unforgettable song "I'm Little But I'm Loud."

We introduced Little Jimmy in the same way that all of our cats are now initiated. He was placed in a locked carrier cage in the middle of our TV room and allowed to be discovered by the others.

It didn't take long. Our resident cats knew we had lost our senses—again! Thank you, but things were quite comfortable the way they were. Maybe the caged thing would just go away.

A half hour later (after all of the cats finished snitting and hissing), I opened the carrier door. Jimmy wasn't about to do anything stupid like venture outside.

As usual, Jerry was the bravest, most playful cat of all. He was the first to make contact with the stranger . . .

. . . and the first to be rewarded with a new playmate.

Welcome to the Cats' House

Rather auspiciously, in 1986, the Chinese Year of the Tiger, Frances and I moved to our present location. Western Hills is a quiet, friendly neighborhood, a nice kind of place to bring up a family of cats. Three generations of Frances's family have lived in this mid-1950s house, a 1,500-square-foot tract home built on a hill overlooking San Diego's sparkling Mission Bay. On a typical clear day, you can see the ocean, if you are a giraffe standing on our roof.

Previously, Frances and I changed residences so regularly that every two years we would automatically pick up cats and relocate again. But this move was different, because we were different. Frances and I finally realized that, with each passing day, we had fewer opportunities to do and say what was important to us. We decided it was time to settle down and admit that our family would always be felines.

With a home of our own, we were now able to consider how we could best fulfill our family's needs. After years of experience as cat watchers, there was one thing Frances and I knew for certain: Felines possess a natural inclination for pleasure and deserve a stimulating environment. We hoped that, with a little remodeling, our almost-bay-view home would also become our cats' lofty playhouse.

The Room Divided

Two hundred and seventy-nine turns . . . Frances and I twisted four hundred feet of pink-dyed sisal around and around the wooden support. After many calluses, it was a wrap. The cat column/room divider was ready for action. We hoped they would use it.

Almost one year after our move, Frances and I decided to separate our living room from its adjoining dining area. Additionally, we wanted to provide a furniture-shredding substitute for our cats' always-needing-to-be-sharpened claws.

Our all-in-one solution was to construct a floor-to-ceiling scratching post that would also provide support for a suspended leaded glass window. In this way, the two rooms would be divided (yet feel open because of the window's transparency), and, most importantly, our cats would have something else to shred.

Almost immediately, we noticed a change in our cats' attitudes. Ground-level travel was now considered beneath them. It was only for those who *had* to walk on the floor. The new structure became their complete activity center—the preferred area for catnapping, attention-seeking, hiding from scary sounds, and game-playing. Their full-speed chases would lead straight to the scratching post. In rapid order, the cats would leap onto the column, dash upward to the supporting beam, race across it, and then come screeching to a stop. Dead end. There was nowhere else to go.

Many people are still trying to solve the riddle of the rope: If the rope circles continuously around the column, how does the beam connect to it? It's simple: Countersink two L-supports into the column; wrap your rope; countersink and attach the beam to the supports; fill in; paint. And presto, the joint is invisible!

Welcome to the Cats' House

Compulsive Completists

It's time to confess: Frances and I are collectors. Whether it's cats or ethnic folk art, we seem to be obsessive—the kind of people who cannot rest until we possess an entire collection.

Even our interior paint colors are done to excess. Over forty colors have been used to enhance the setting for our ever-expanding collection of Central and South American crafts. We're on our way to featuring every color in the book. In fact, we've had to extend our paint search to Mexico to obtain many of the distinctive, saturated colors that are hard to find in the United States. Hot pink is not used very often in American homes!

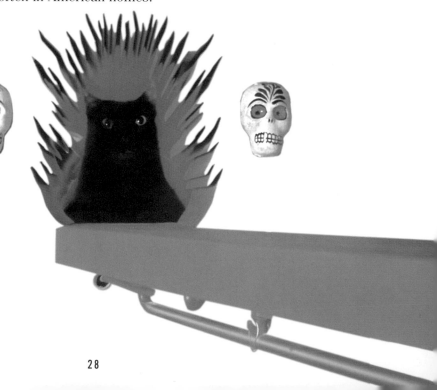

For several years, our collecting efforts have concentrated on the arts of Mexico; primarily, the figures and toys associated with Días de los Muertos (Days of the Dead). Many people confuse the skeletal figures of Días de los Muertos with those of Halloween—the scary evening when adults act out their fantasies, and spooks and goblins go bump in the night.

In contrast, Días de los Muertos is an occasion for family and community to come together to express the continuance of life, demonstrate love and respect for one's ancestors, and reaffirm family relationships.

Cats
Overhead!

Literally, one thing led to the next. Adding a
second entry/exit was necessary to complete
the loop so that our cats could avoid being
cornered. The new section initiated a series
of expansions that now allows the catwalkers
to travel on more than one-hundred feet of
elevated home highway.

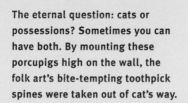

The eternal question: cats or possessions? Sometimes you can have both. By mounting these porcupigs high on the wall, the folk art's bite-tempting toothpick spines were taken out of cat's way.

Cats and people don't always see eye to eye. In designing the catwalk, I've made certain that anywhere the cats can get to, I can get to, too. (Helpful when rounding up cats for vet visits.)

A cat's-eye-view from the top of our coat closet: here the living room walkway connects with the TV room and hallway pathways. The centralized hub provides weary catwalkers with a spacious rest area—and sanctuary from children and other loud noises.

Welcome to the Cats' House

Fur Flies Down

Leaving our coat closet's red-illuminated interior behind, catwalkers pass through a cat-sized mouse hole to enter our TV/reading room. This colorful activity center is, without a doubt, our felines' favorite area. When Frances and I are viewing television, the cats are usually warming our laps or playing over our heads. It's not unusual for us to witness fur floating down in front of our screen.

For years, Frances and I have heard that cats are independent creatures. Our experience suggests otherwise: Wherever we are, they want to be, too. Why display your latest acrobatic maneuvers in a remote room where no one is around to be impressed?

Welcome to the Cats' House

Architectural details were kept to a minimum so attention could be focused on the most important part of the walkway—our cats.

Thankfully, during the early stages of construction, Frances and I learned an important design lesson. We observed how difficult it was for the cats to turn around on the walkway if their path hugged the wall.

To reverse direction, the cats were forced to put their heads between their rear legs and perform a contortionist flip (an impossible feat for our larger felines). Now, turn-around space is always included in the final design.

Welcome to the Cats' House

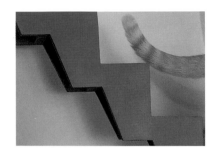

"Benjamin Bunny" was advanced in his years when the catwalk construction began. Maturity had made him a little stiff in the joints and wisely respectful of his limitations. Racing up floor-to-ceiling columns was not the kind of daredevil thrill that appealed to our Bunny's sensibilities. Once up, it was too difficult for him to get back down. He needed stairs.

The twenty-three step, spiral staircase was designed to provide Benjamin with an easy, alternative access to the seven-foot-high walkway. However, Frances and I quickly discovered that what was good for our Bunny was even better for the friskier felines. Our speedsters find great fun in racing up and down the sharply curved stairs.

Welcome to the Cats' House

Calafia's Triangle

Calafia is the leader of our sleepers. In fact, none of our felines even comes close to equaling her ability to discover—and steadfastly retain—the latest, best place for napping.

It has been reported that cats sleep, on the average, sixteen hours per day. Rest assured, Calafia is not average. Soon after we first installed the catwalk's triangular passageway, Frances and I became worried that a mysterious power had taken possession of Calafia. For three weeks, she would only descend from the triangle's grasp when floor-level activities necessitated. Then, Calafia would hurriedly complete her chores and race back to her lofty bed.

Frances and I have been asked if our felines ever fall off of the catwalk. The answer is: yes. Sometimes they attempt speeds and movements that are beyond even their grasp. But the most frequent reason for our cats' infrequent falls is that they become forgetful. A toss, a turn, and a rude awakening quickly refreshes their memory—no longer are they sleeping on the six-inch-wide walkway. So far, there haven't been any serious injuries. Thankfully, generations of curious cats have genetically enabled ours to land on their feet.

As a finishing detail, we wanted to incorporate one of our carved wooden snakes into the triangle's design. But there was a problem. None of our snakes were long enough to span the intended distance.

The solution was easy: cut the snake into two parts and place a half at each end of the passageway. Our rambunctious cats thought that was terrific. Now the snake was bite-size and easily transportable—it never rested again. (An interior design tip: Always nail your snake.)

Welcome to the Cats' House

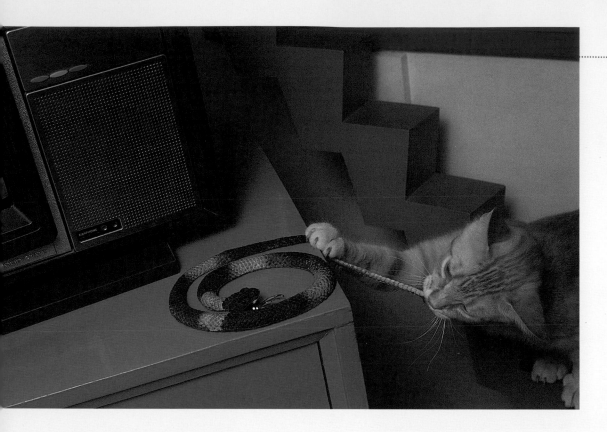

Only the boldest bugs, rodents, and
rubber snakes venture into our cats'
house. Those foolish enough to enter
risk encountering TomCat, our ever-
vigilant protector from unwanted
intruders.

Snake Attack

Snakes can be sneaky. Just when they seem defenseless they attack and catch you off guard. Tom will return another day to defeat this one.

Onward
and Outward

Soon we'll be able to say: "The cat's in the mail" (well, actually, mailbox). Currently, the TV-room walkway splits at mid-ceiling: one path travels down Benjamin's spiral stairs to floor level; and the second extends through Calafia's Triangle, terminating at a mailbox mounted high on the wall adjoining the backyard.

Our inside cats are looking forward to also being outside cats. Plans are in the works for the mailbox to become the gateway to a screened playground/nature preserve. Our felines will be pampered with special areas for bird-watching, sunning, frolicking, exploring, and, of course, catting around on the latest in elevated walkways.

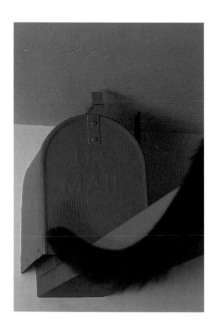

Our mailbox was sawed into three sections and incorporated into the catwalk. It now serves as a lockable passageway to the backyard and as the two mouse hole openings into the coat closet.

Frances and I couldn't just stop at the TV/reading room—more rooms were still available! Onward our elevated journey continued to the twinkling stars of the Milky Way and beyond, through the twisting path of our neon hallway.

^A Hallway How-To

Through a succession of stud-finder scans, wall thumps, drilled holes, and finger pokes, I eventually located the hidden electrical wiring and 2 x 4 supports. Using a keyhole saw, I was able to cut my opening (carefully avoiding the wiring) along the wall's top and vertical support beams.

I must admit, it was invigorating when I cut out my first mouse hole. During childhood, most of us are taught to not make large openings in our walls. However (as someone who experiences lapses of adulthood), when I was faced with another opportunity to cut into our wall, I was excited. This time, a bigger challenge was needed to ignite my imagination—flames! Mouse holes were a piece of cheese by now.

Once again, our centralized coat closet became the point of departure for our cats' new walkway and opening. Its red-illuminated interior would provide a perfect, glowing background for a flame-shaped opening.

Once you've accepted color into your life (and cats overhead), it would be disappointing to return to off-white walls (and felines at your feet).

In a zigzag path, nineteen feet of ruby red neon lead our cats down the hallway—through fiery flames to the golden pyramid of Quetzalcoatl.

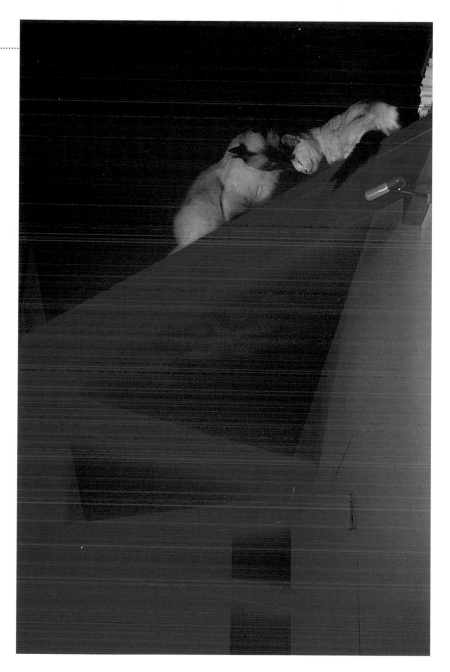

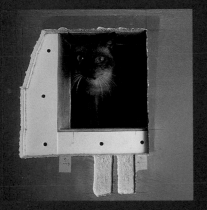

For the second stage of construction, a wood-L was made with a 2 x 4 and attached with screws to the wall's support beams. Next, I filled the gap between the 2 x 4 support and the hallway wall with stiff cardboard and routed grooves to receive the walkway's supports. Finally, the inner wall of the closet was removed to open the passageway for Benjamin's inspection.

Being careful to keep the two steel supports level to each other, I mounted the 4" L-brackets into the prerouted grooves with toggle bolts. Next, my precut (and prerouted) 2 x 6 Douglas fir board was screwed to the supports. The new section was ready to support even the heaviest of domestic TomCats.

Before my flames could be cut out, I had to combine wood. Six pieces of 1 x 10 x 10 poplar wood were glued and bar-clamped together. Using a band saw, I trimmed the large block of wood to fit the opening and thickness of our wall.

Next, I sawed the block in half so that the interior flames could be cut out. By removing small sections at a time, I was able to follow the intricate pattern without any problems. Then, care-fully. . . the flames were fastened into the wall opening with nails.

Now, only some routing and the final stages of surface finishing remained. A handheld grinder was used to rout approximately $\frac{1}{8}$" of the front wood surface area, leaving a raised lip around the inside edge of the flames. This allowed the fill plaster to seam-lessly feather so that the flames would appear to be cut out of the wall.

Welcome to the Cats' House

After only a few minutes (actually, many days) of final wall prepping, plastering, sanding, plastering, sanding, painting, hanging, and neon installation . . . the flames were ready to engulf Joseph.

Welcome to the Cats' House

Pyramid
of the Sun

A long time ago, in the second century B.C., the people of Teotihuacán, Mexico, commenced construction of a great pyramid. Rising to a height of 206 feet, the Pyramid of the Sun has been described as the most impressive building of Ancient America. It is believed that the pyramid served as a center of worship to Quetzalcoatl, the Aztec god of the sky and wind, the creative forces, and the Breath of Life.

In all probability, the ancient monuments could have been built much faster if felines had been allowed to help. Our eager assistants involved themselves in every phase of the pyramid's construction.

To exit the hallway, our catwalkers pass through an Aztec star embedded in their own gold-leafed Pyramid of the Sun.

Enticing us to reach upward, our felines stay temptingly out of touch. For us, it's a numbing exercise in futility. When we've lost all mobility in our blood-drained fingers, they swiftly attack. It's not fair. They have the advantage when we have an upper hand.

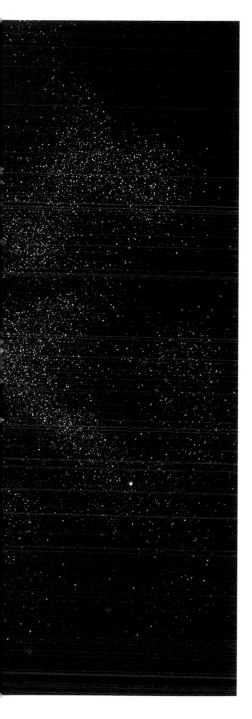

Overhead are rhinestones representing the constellations and souls of Quetzalcoatl's followers. It was believed that when his worshippers left this earthly existence they arose to become the stars in the night sky.

57

The
Perfect Fit

We discovered that by expanding feline access vertically to the walls and overhead, more cats could be accommodated more comfortably, all within the same but expanded space. It didn't take us long to fill the new space. Our family of cats grew rapidly, both in quantity and in physical size. (Several people have suggested that our cats could lose a little weight.)

TomCat is one of our big-boned guys. After a full meal, he volunteered to demonstrate that wall openings aren't just made—they're the result of careful measurements of our most wide-bodied cats.

Jerry Lee is demonstrating how easy it is for a pitiful, recently bathed kitten to pass through the star-opening into our bedroom. (The missing fur and cut above his right eye occurred during one of his many losing attacks on our sleeping cats.)

On the other paw, TomCat is proving
that tubby tabbies can make it through,
too. And who was it that said stripes
are slimming? Perhaps if the stripes
went the other direction . . .

Welcome to the Cats' House

Cats-Only Clubhouse

Passing through the star, our sky travelers continue their journey into the bedroom. Immediately, they reach their most exclusive site—our clothes closet. From the entryway, the closet looks like millions of others that have chartreuse-painted doors. Not until you pass it does anything look unusual: A mouse-shaped skull-and-crossbones opening is carved into the closet's side wall.

Carefully drawing closer, the visitor can see that the cryptic opening provides passage into the Cats-Only Clubhouse—an eerie green illuminated room built into the top of the closet. This is our cats' private retreat, their place to kick legs into the air, let fur down, and swap tails. Absolutely no mice are allowed inside.

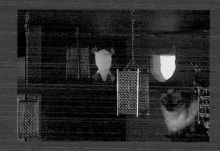

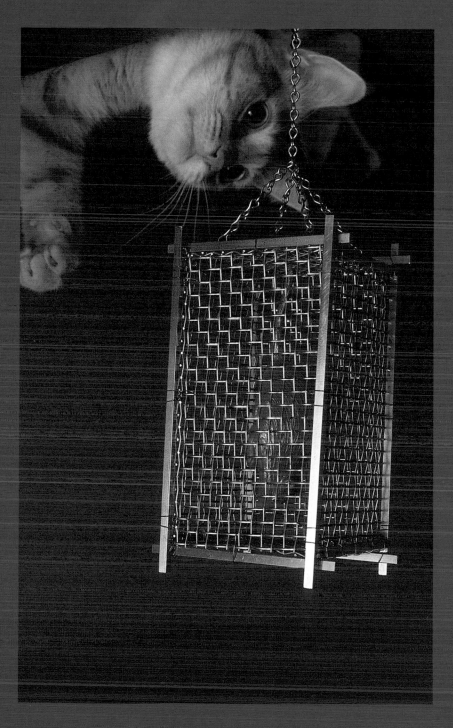

Three brass cages are suspended by chains from the ceiling—in each, a mouse effigy dangles by its tail. The warnings are not intended to be subtle. Any rodents daring to trespass are forewarned: This area is a mouse-free zone and intruders will become entertainment.

Welcome to the Cats' House

A large, watchful TomCat cutout looms over the cages and adjoining TV/reading room. Tom was quite pleased to have a wall opening modeled after his own image. Even his whiskers were cut out allowing light to shine through them.

From the bedroom, our camouflaged cats are able to secretly watch everyone's activities in the living and television rooms (just as villains in mystery movies do when they peer through eyeholes in paintings).

Welcome to the Cats' House

Advice on the Incline

Leaving their mice dangling, our catwalkers continue their venture to the path's final precipice, follow its steep descent, and, fittingly, come to rest on our bed. This is how they wanted their walkway to end. But, to be honest, it's not what I had intended for them.

Originally, I planned to build an extraordinary, spiraling staircase that would rival an architect's best endeavor. Fortuitously, our cats showed me an easier path. I had installed a temporary, short ramp from our dresser to the overhead walkway. Immediately our frisky felines were racing fleetly up and down their new ramp (except for when they would lose their grip and frantically claw for traction).

Quickly, I scrapped my elegant spiral design and instead constructed a sixteen-foot, wall-to-wall ramp. Along the incline's 30-degree slope, red carpeting was recessed to fix the footing problem. Now, our cats enjoy high-speed access to their aerial highway and are equipped with the latest in carpeted scratching ramps.

Of course, our cats would prefer that their walkway extend even further. But they're grateful for what they've got—and they hope their fellow felines will be rewarded with catwalks, too.

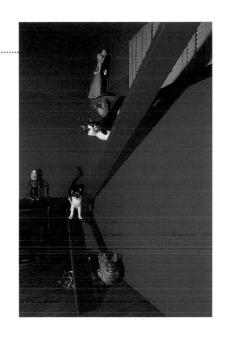

Welcome to the Cats' House

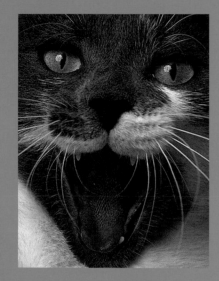

Your
Cats
Will

Let's face it, we all want to make our cats happy—that's what we're here for. Every day at feeding time, they're there for us. When we need to pet a cat or have our laps warmed, they will usually oblige. After all of their sacrifices, the least we can do is rearrange our furniture. Move things around a little. Create steps to the tops of those hard-to-jump-to cupboards and bookshelves. It's a part of their nature: Cats love to look down on us.

Thank You

A Matter
of Placement

Be sensible when remodeling. Don't position your cat's lofty new lookout next to the curtains—a favorite ladder used by felines worldwide. Also (as if it needs to be mentioned), move your treasured possessions out of cat's way. Most felines are amazingly surefooted creatures. However, for those of us with clumsier cats . . . a kit of white glue, masking tape, and rubber bands will hold together and mend many broken belongings.

Seasons change and bring new opportunities. Good designers need to be visionaries—to be able to look into the future and anticipate the consequences of their placement decisions.

What would we do without their assistance? Periodically, Jimmy performs a safety check to verify that the L-screws are still securely holding our skeletal musicians.

Over the years, Frances and I have found a variety of solutions that enable us to safeguard our folk art collection. (Or, more accurately, we "affix" it—nothing is ever really safe.)

For smaller and midsize items, we use Quake Hold™ to attach our collectibles to tabletops and shelves. It's a flexible putty that is a twist to use. You simply put a few dabs of the putty under your artwork, give it a slight turn, and presto, your treasured item is protected from cat-shakes. To remove, you give the artwork a slight reverse turn, lift it off, and peel off the putty. Quake Hold™ holds—just don't expect miracles. (Direct cat hits will send almost anything flying.)

Sometimes heavy-duty solutions are required. Frances and I have been known to drill holes into our tables and lamps and mount them with bolts. But if it's a fragile piece of artwork that we're trying to protect, then we attach its base to the display surface with plastic tube–covered L-screws and wait to see if any of the artwork's appendages (like arms or legs) will be knocked off by careless cats.

Your Cats Will Thank You

The Necessary Attitude

A long time ago, Frances and I decided to not cry over spilled milk, broken folk art, or bitten plants. Why allow ourselves to be upset over the inevitable? Cats will be cats, and we'll be happier if we don't fret the occasional loss.

Instead of trying to change our cats, we changed our furnishings. Now, our couches are covered with plastic. Never in our wildest dreams did Frances and I think that we would do that! At least the covers come off when visitors arrive (well, at least for their first visit). Good friends know to dress for plastic and not to bring flowers.

During these stressful times, the least we can do for our felines is to help them face the midday sun. We've all witnessed the cat-cleansing effects of sunshine: the melted muscles, exposed bellies, and not-a-care-in-the-world reveries.

Perfect sunning window

Recently, Frances improved our cats' quality of life. She purchased a used shelf unit at an antique store, refinished it, and then, with my assistance, mounted it on our sunbathed kitchen's wall—a perfect location. Now, if we could only find a way to keep the cats out of the bathroom blinds . . .

Imperfect sunning window

Your Cats Will Thank You

The Voice
of Experience

Most cats won't be satisfied with just a sun shelf. They'll need a higher platform—an overhead path to keep them one step above you. Take it from someone who has built one: The decision to elevate your cat's life will have you living with plaster particles for months.

However, as a seasoned pro, I can show you how I solved the dust problem. For one and a half years, the routing and sanding of our walls covered every room in our house with plaster dust. One day I had the brilliant idea to create a small, sealed room out of plastic sheeting. I could get in, rout my grooves, and, for once, keep the pervasive dust inside.

The instant that I turned on the router, my room filled completely with dust and the oxygen escaped, making the plastic suck in . . . I couldn't breathe or see . . . had to grope my way to the edge . . . ripped open the taped plastic sheeting (allowing all of the trapped plaster dust to escape) . . . and lived to offer this sagely advice: Before you begin, cover your furniture.

How to
Get Overhead

Our cats think that your cats should be upwardly mobile. To make ascension a little easier, the Cats' House cats would like to share construction perspectives with you for their cat column, carpeted ramp, and spiral staircase. Each of these climbing devices have been feline-tested and found to be enjoyable by cats of all ages. However, elderly and de-clawed cats may have difficulty descending the cat column. (An easy solution: build a ramp and stairway, too.)

3/8"

1 1/2"

5 1/2"

5/16"

Inclined Ramp

Making our cats' carpeted ramp was a snap. Grooves were routed into two pieces of 2 x 6 douglas fir so that the unsightly edges of the carpet could be countersunk. Then, the sections of wood were cut to fit, attached to the walls and floor with L-brackets, and painted. Finally, to provide traction for our speedsters, red looped carpeting was glued into the ramp's grooves.

To make the cat column's installation easier, a floor-to-ceiling length, three-sided box was constructed out of 1 x 6 pine. The removeable fourth side made it simple to get inside and attach the column to the ceiling with a toggle-bolt, and to our hardwood floor with screws. In final preparation for ascent and claw sharpening, pink-dyed $\frac{3}{8}$" sisal was wrapped continuously around and attached to the column with fence staples.

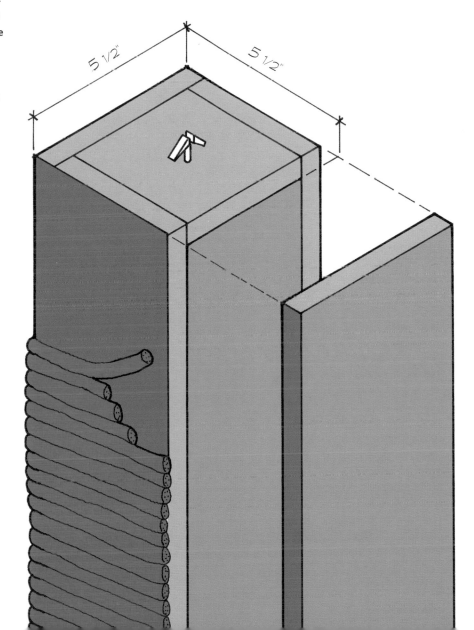

5 1/2"

5 1/2"

Cat Column

For many people, the highlight of the catwalk is Benjamin's spiral staircase. Our felines probably agree. They know that cats look good on circular stairs.

But your flight of stairs doesn't have to be as elaborate. There are lots of ways to get cats overhead. The important thing is to start. Like most endeavors, the hardest part is making that first step. After that, sweeping staircases are easy. Do you want your cats to be left on the ground?

The spiral stairs look cool, but they were not a breeze to make. First, I measured my intended floor-to-catwalk height, and then divided the distance into twenty-three equal steps. Next, the spiral's radius was determined (approximately 110°) so that I could begin designing the staircase's building blocks.

Each particle board step unit was made separately, and later fastened together with bolts and carpenter's glue. I discovered that it's best to build and install the staircase first, and then construct the connecting catwalk afterward (that way every-thing aligns properly). The easiest part was getting our cats to use their new spiral stairway.

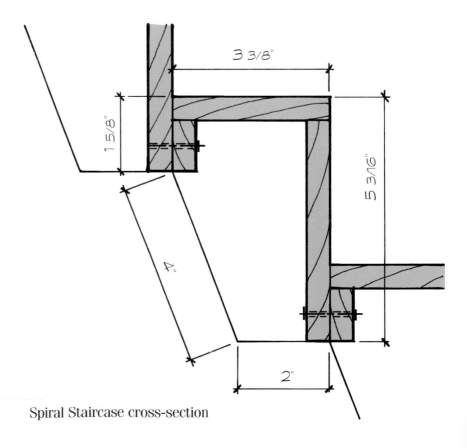

Spiral Staircase cross-section

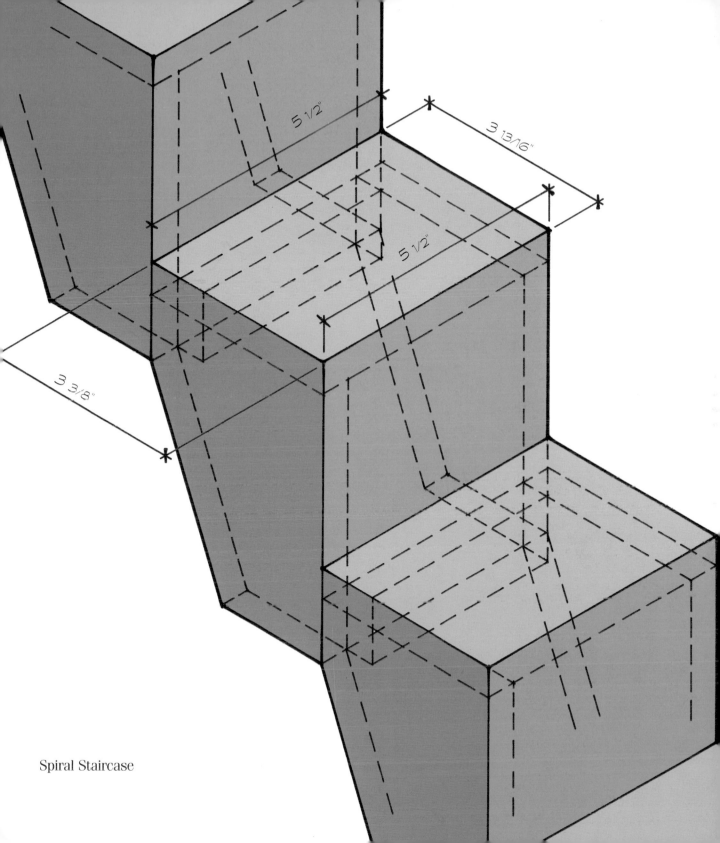

5 1/2"

3 13/16"

5 1/2"

3 3/8"

Spiral Staircase

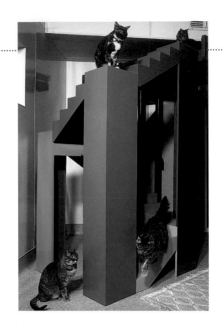

Retirement:
Southern California Style

Each year, Frances and I give up our life of dust and solitude by inviting the public into our home to benefit the National Cat Protection Society. This nonprofit organization has two cat retirement and adoption centers in California that place over two thousand cats each year into qualifying homes.

Recently, the NCPS moved their headquarters to Newport Beach (one block from the ocean) and asked if I would design a cat habitat for their new retirement center. Of course, I quickly said yes. How many times do you get to make waves for cats? Now, thanks to the NCPS and Patrick Kennedy's Construction Company, every day is a day at the beach for these retirement cats.

Your Cats Will Thank You

Karen's cats. She had five! We thought
that was a lot.

Nine

In the seventies, our lives were in balance. Frances and I maintained the perfect, two-cat family. But our friend Karen . . . well, we knew that she was out of control because she had five cats.

Now, Frances and I live with nine cats—more cats than most people ever have in a lifetime. But our friend Karen . . . well, she now has John and an eighteen-feline household. One thing is certain: Frances and I will never have as many cats as Karen!

We have discovered that there are benefits to having large feline families. For heat and health, cats are hard to beat. As soon as we sit or lie down, Frances and I are lovingly cuddled by our cats. They generously apply their therapeutic warmth and rhythmic purrs to our tired muscles. Cats know what's good for us. Scientific studies have

Lives

shown that a friendly purr can calm people's frayed nerves and help them fight off ulcers, strokes, depression, and heart attacks. Just having a cat on your lap and stroking it can lower blood pressure.

Unfortunately, there is a painful disparity between cats and people. On the average, household cats have a life span of twelve years; for people, it's typically six times longer. Too soon, we learn that our loved ones are unable to continue sharing our times together. During these past ten years, Frances and I have had to accept the losses of Beauregard, Benjamin, Calafia, Terri, and Celeste. Everywhere that we look, imprinted throughout *The Cats' House*, are reminders of our shared lives. It seems that heartbreak is the unwanted counterpart to joy. Thankfully, our companions will always be with us, though very much missed.

At this time, nine cats seems to be the right amount—any more than that might make it harder for us to know them as individuals. But at what point do we close the door? There are so many deserving cats that need good homes. Frances and I have made a personal policy of adopting only from shelters. We've found that life's abandoned cats can easily capture our hearts and provide years of loving companionship.

And . . . what years they've been! Frances and I still find it amazing that such a simple act, like altering our house to accommodate the needs of our companions, could so completely alter our lives as well.

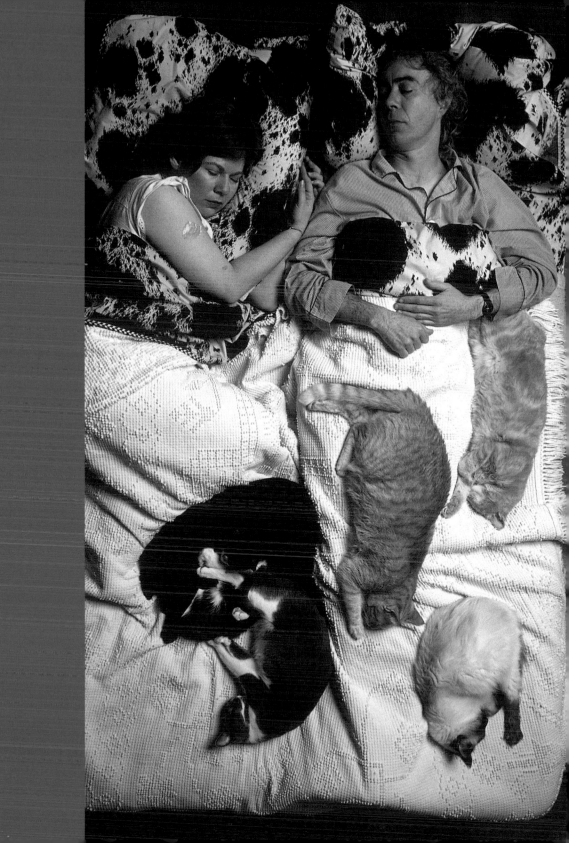

Acknowledgments

**Sometimes, a helping hand
is needed. . . .**

For the past ten years, the Cats' House has captivated my thoughts and actions, tested relationships, demanded discovery of inner resources, and limited Frances's and my livelihood. Now I know what other authors know: Creating a book is a lot of work and an indescribable delight. If I'm fortunate enough to find a second book within me . . . in another month, I will eagerly begin anew. But today I need to thank those that made my first effort possible.

It's gratifying to witness "Bob Walker" on the front cover, but I can assure you, *The Cats' House* was not a solo effort. It was a collaboration by countless individuals who offered the encouragement, suggestions, and skills that allowed for my concept to progress to completion.

My best friend, Frances Mooney, and mother-in-law, Estelle Mooney, cannot be thanked enough. Their steadfast support provided the foundation for my vision to be realized. *The Cats' House* is dedicated to them.

Before I had a book proposal, I had Laurie Fox. She worked for me and was unmercifully forced to learn the dreaded computer. Later, she became an agent for the Linda Chester Literary Agency and gently helped me become an author. Thankfully, I didn't get back what I gave to her. Without Laurie's and Linda's nurturing assistance I would not have found my publisher, Andrews and McMeel. Thank you!

It was a perfect match. Andrews and McMeel has so many cat-owned people on staff that *The Cats' House* instantly felt at home there. In fact, my two-cat editor, Kathy Viele, has more poundage of animals living with her than Frances and I will ever have in our lifetimes! My manuscript couldn't have found a more supportive publishing team: Kathy's masterly guidance; the insightful copyediting of Matt Lombardi; and the production wizardry of Katie Mace, Traci Bertz, and Jonna Sherman.

Again, I would like to thank Andrews and McMeel for the trust and creative freedom that they placed in me and Tyler Blik Design. San Diego's award-winning design group was able to endure my input and still make a book as elegant as I had hoped for. Thank you for making my cats so perfect on their pages: Tyler Blik, Ron Fleming, Jennifer Carlenzoli, Gary Benzel, and Ken Soto.

One of the pleasures that *The Cats' House* project has produced is Frances's and my association with the National Cat Protection Society. Their organization has become "the source" for our cats and our catalyst for housecleaning: Over 2,000 NCPS supporters have herded through our annual Open Cat Houses. Thanks a lot!

Finally, I have to admit that *The Cats' House* benefited from additional efforts that were beyond my abilities: artist/ architectural illustrator Mario Lara provided the floorplan blueprints and the perspective drawings on pages 78-81; Frances Mooney took the photographs of me on page 76 and the back interior dust jacket; Katherine Mooney and Frances Mooney designed Pop's devotional altar, page 29; and Tim Bee, Sam Nakamura, and Dennis Reiter of Chrome (my trustworthy photo lab) guaranteed that this

photographic project would be professional.

It would take another book to thank all of the people and organizations that have influenced and contributed to this project. In advance, I must apologize for any unintentional omissions. Thank you for making *The Cats' House* possible:

James & Helen Ard; Margaret Ard; Isaac Artenstein; Lee Austen; David & Ruthie Bales; Joseph Bellows; John Bergstreser; Arthur & Helena Brugman; Gerri Calore; Barbara Carbuhn; Shannon Carroll; David Covey; Kay, Margie, & Sarah Crosbie; Tim & Sherry Crump; Dennis, Barbara, Christine, & Andrew Culleton; Frank Daniels; Omer Divers; Joan, Brian, & Erin Dougherty; Jude Eberhard; James & Jennifer Esquivel; Dave Garcia, Louis Goldich; Grossmont College Photo Club; John & Laura Cunningham Hilbig; Marie Hill & Fredrick Hill Jr.; Melinda Holden; Suda House; Hyde Gallery; Tom Jacobson; Denise Johnston; Harry Kaczur; Kay Kaiser; John Kalpus; Sheila Keifetz; Patrick Kennedy; Dillon Kerekes; David Kinney;

Edith Kodmur; Mario Lara; Tom Lazzara; Mary Beth Link; Mark-Elliot Lugo; Jim & Janet Madden; Teresa Markey; Douglas McClure; Ron, Sandy, Derrick, & Brian McPherson; Patrick Miller; Wayne & Nora Miller; Sumner & Elinor Mitchell; John & Estelle Mooney; Katherine Mooney; Nancy Mooney; John Moore; Museum of Photographic Arts; Allwyn O'Mara; Christine Oatman; Arthur Ollman; Tom & Cathy Redel; Pat Rose; Robert Schneider; Marge Sheldon; David Raphael Singer; Norman Sizemore; Ron Snyder; Carrie Soler; Paul Stamm; John Stephens; Bruce, Suzie, Stacey, Kimberly, Leslie, & Melissa Stoll; Edith Stoll; Jan & Linda Tonnesen; Karen Truax; Hitoshi & Terri Tsuchida; Chuck Valverde; Watts Color Lab; Jean Ellen Wilder; Jim Wilsterman; David Wing; and, of course, the Cats' House cats.

And, last but not least . . . I know it's a trite thing to say, but thank you Mom and Dad for making *my* efforts possible.